SCHOLASTIC

READ & RESPOND

Bringing the best books to life in the classroom

Activities based on Winnie the Witch

By Valerie Thomas and Korky Paul

CW01645495

Terms and conditions

IMPORTANT – PERMITTED USE AND WARNINGS – READ CAREFULLY BEFORE USING

Save for these purposes, or as expressly authorised in the accompanying materials, the software may not be copied, reproduced, used, sold, licensed, transferred, exchanged, hired, or exported in whole or in part or in any manner or form without the prior written consent of Scholastic Ltd. Any such unauthorised use or activities are prohibited and may give rise to civil liabilities and criminal prosecutions.

The material contained on this CD-ROM may only be used in the context for which it was intended in *Read & Respond,* and is for use only by the purchaser or purchasing institution that has purchased the book and CD-ROM. Permission to download images is given for purchasers only and not for users from any lending service. Any further use of the material contravenes Scholastic Ltd's copyright and that of other rights holders.

This CD-ROM has been tested for viruses at all stages of its production. However, we recommend that you run virus-checking software on your computer systems at all times. Scholastic Ltd cannot accept any responsibility for any loss, disruption or damage to your data or your computer system that may occur as a result of using either the CD-ROM or the data held on it.

IF YOU ACCEPT THE ABOVE CONDITIONS YOU MAY PROCEED TO USE THE CD-ROM.

Recommended system requirements:
Windows: XP (Service Pack 3), Vista (Service Pack 2), Windows 7 or Windows 8 with 2.33GHz processor
Mac: OS 10.6 to 10.8 with Intel Core™ Duo processor
1GB RAM (recommended)
1024 x 768 Screen resolution
CD-ROM drive (24x speed recommended)
Adobe Reader (version 9 recommended for Mac users)
Broadband internet connections (for installation and updates)

For all technical support queries (including no CD drive), please phone Scholastic Customer Services on 0845 6039091.

Designed using Adobe Indesign
Published by Scholastic Education, an imprint of Scholastic Ltd
Book End, Range Road, Witney, Oxfordshire, OX29 0YD
Registered office: Westfield Road, Southam, Warwickshire CV47 0RA

Printed and bound by Ashford Colour Press

1 2 3 4 5 6 7 8 9 6 7 8 9 0 1 2 3 4 5

British Library Cataloguing-in-Publication Data
A catalogue record for this book is available from the British Library.
ISBN 978-1407-16066-5

Author Samantha Pope
Editorial team Rachel Morgan, Jenny Wilcox, Lucy Tritton and Vicky Butt
Series designer Neil Salt
Designer Anna Oliwa
Illustrator Gemma Hastilow
Digital development Hannah Barnett, Phil Crothers and MWA Technologies Private Ltd

Acknowledgements
The publishers gratefully acknowledge permission to reproduce the following copyright material:

Oxford University Press for the use of the cover and extracts from *Winnie the Witch* written by Valerie Thomas and illustrated by Korky Paul (OUP, 2012). Text copyright © Valerie Thomas 1987, illustrations copyright © Korky Paul 1987. Used by permission of the publishers, Oxford University Press.

Every effort has been made to trace copyright holders for the works reproduced in this book, and the publishers apologise for any inadvertent omissions.

CONTENTS

INTRODUCTION

Read & Respond provides teaching ideas related to a specific children's book. The series focuses on best-loved books and brings you ways to use them to engage your class and enthuse them about reading.

The book is divided into different sections:

- **About the book and author:** gives you some background information about the book and the author.
- **Guided reading:** breaks the book down into sections and gives notes for using it with guided reading groups. A bookmark has been provided on page 10 containing comprehension questions. The children can be directed to refer to these as they read.
- **Shared reading:** provides extracts from the children's book with associated notes for focused work. There is also one non-fiction extract that relates to the children's book.
- **Phonics & spelling:** provides phonics and spelling work related to the children's book so you can teach these skills in context.
- **Plot, character & setting:** contains activity ideas focused on the plot, characters and the setting of the story.
- **Talk about it:** has speaking and listening activities related to the children's book. These activities may be based directly on the children's book or be broadly based on the themes and concepts of the story.
- **Get writing:** provides writing activities related to the children's book. These activities may be based directly on the children's book or be broadly based on the themes and concepts of the story.
- **Assessment:** contains short activities that will help you assess whether the children have understood concepts and curriculum objectives. They are designed to be informal activities to feed into your planning.

The activities follow the same format:

- **Objective:** the objective for the lesson. It will be based upon a curriculum objective, but will often be more specific to the focus being covered.
- **What you need:** a list of resources you need to teach the lesson, including digital resources (printable pages, interactive activities and media resources, see page 5).
- **What to do:** the activity notes.
- **Differentiation:** this is provided where specific and useful differentiation advice can be given to support and/or extend the learning in the activity. Differentiation by providing additional adult support has not been included as this will be at a teacher's discretion based upon specific children's needs and ability, as well as the availability of support.

The activities are numbered for reference within each section and should move through the text sequentially – so you can use the lesson while you are reading the book. Once you have read the book, most of the activities can be used in any order you wish.

Below are brief guidance notes for using the CD-ROM. For more detailed information, please click on the '?' button in the top right-hand corner of the screen.

The program contains the following:

- the extract pages from the book
- all of the photocopiable pages from the book
- additional printable pages
- interactive on-screen activities
- media resources.

Getting started

Put the CD-ROM into your CD-ROM drive. If you do not have a CD-ROM drive, phone Scholastic Customer Services on 0845 6039091.

- For Windows users, the install wizard should autorun. If it fails to do so, then navigate to your CD-ROM drive and follow the installation process.
- For Mac users, copy the disk image file to your hard drive. After it has finished copying, double click it to mount the disk image. Navigate to the mounted disk image and run the installer. After installation, the disk image can be unmounted and the DMG can be deleted from the hard drive.
- To install on a network, see the ReadMe file located on the CD-ROM (navigate to your drive).

To complete the installation of the program you need to open the program and click 'Update' in the pop-up. Please note – this CD-ROM is web-enabled and the content will be downloaded from the internet to your hard drive to populate the CD-ROM with the relevant resources. This only needs to be done on first use. After this, you will be able to use the CD-ROM without an internet connection. If at any point any content is updated, you will receive another pop-up upon start-up when there is an internet connection.

Main menu

The main menu is the first screen that appears. Here you can access: terms and conditions, registration links, how to use the CD-ROM and credits. To access a specific book click on the relevant button (NB only titles installed will be available). You can filter by the drop-down lists if you wish. You can search all resources by clicking 'Search' in the bottom left-hand corner. You can also log in and access favourites that you have bookmarked.

Resources

By clicking on a book on the Main menu, you are taken to the resources for that title. The resources are: Media, Interactives, Extracts and Printables. Select the category and then launch a resource by clicking the play button.

Teacher settings

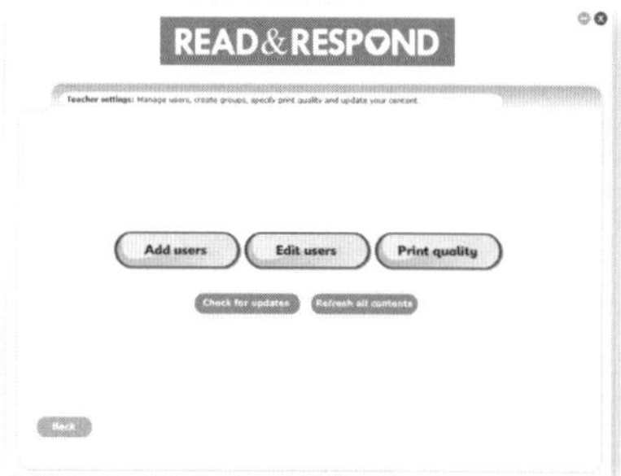

In the top right-hand corner of the screen is a small 'T' icon. This is the teacher settings area. It is password protected. The password is: login. This area will allow you to choose the print quality settings for interactive activities ('Default' or 'Best') and also allow you to check for updates to the program or re-download all content to the disk via 'Refresh all content'. You can also set up user logins so that you can save and access favourites. Once a user is set up, they can enter by clicking the login link underneath the 'T' and '?' buttons.

Search

You can access an all resources search by clicking the search button on the bottom-left of the Main menu. You can search for activities by type (using the drop-down filter) or by keyword by typing into the box. You can then assign resources to your favourites area or launch them directly from the search area.

CURRICULUM LINKS

Section	Activity	Curriculum objectives
Guided reading		Comprehension: To discuss the significance of the title and events in a book; to make inferences on the basis of what is being said and done.
Shared reading	1	Composition: To learn how to use both familiar and new punctuation correctly including full stops, capital letters, exclamation marks and commas.
	2	Transcription: To add the suffux 'ed' where no change is needed to the root word.
	3	Comprehension: To develop understanding by listening to, discussing and expressing views.
Phonics & spelling	1	Word reading: To read words with contractions and understand that the apostrophe represents the omitted letter(s).
	2	Transcription: To add 'es' or 's' to nouns to make plurals.
	3	Transcription: To add 'er' and 'est' to adjectives where no change is needed in the spelling of root words.
	4	Word reading: To understand the division of words into syllables.
Plot, character & setting	1	Comprehension: To predict what might happen from details stated and implied.
	2	Comprehension: To link what they read to their own experiences.
	3	Comprehension: To discuss their understanding of books.
	4	Comprehension: To explain clearly their understanding of what is read to them.
	5	Comprehension: To participate in discussion about books, taking turns and listening to what others say.
	6	Comprehension: To discuss the sequence of events in books.
Talk about it	1	Spoken language: To participate actively in collaborative conversations, staying on topic and initiating and responding to comments.
	2	Spoken language: To listen and respond appropriately to others; to use relevant strategies to build their vocabulary.
	3	Spoken language: To participate in discussions, performances and role play.
	4	Spoken language: To give well-structured descriptions, including for expressing feelings.
	5	Spoken language: To articulate and justify answers, arguments and opinions.
	6	Spoken language: To participate in discussions and presentations.
Get writing	1	Composition: To plan or say out loud what they are going to write about.
	2	Composition: To use expanded noun phrases to describe and specify.
	3	Composition: To compose a sentence orally before writing it.
	4	Composition: To use subordination ('when', 'if', 'that' or 'because') and coordination (using 'or', 'and' or 'but').
	5	Composition: To plan or say out loud what they are going to write about.
	6	Composition: To punctuate sentences using a capital letter and a full stop.
Assessment	1	Comprehension: To explain clearly their understanding of what is read to them.
	2	Composition: To punctuate sentences using a capital letter and a full stop.
	3	Transcription: To spell by learning to spell more words with contracted forms.
	4	Transcription: To add the suffux 'ed' where no change is needed to the root word.

About the book

The first book in the popular *Winnie the Witch* series, which has sold more than five million copies worldwide, introduces us to the loveable but accident-prone witch, Winnie, and her loyal and long-suffering cat, Wilbur. Winnie likes dressing in bright colours and is especially found of her stripy yellow and orange socks. However, everything in her house is black, including the furniture and soft furnishings. In fact, everything is so dark that she can only see her poor black cat Wilbur if his eyes are open; when he's asleep Winnie is liable to trip over him or sit on him. One day, Winnie comes up with a plan to solve the problem, but whatever she does brings with it a whole new set of problems!

About the author

Valerie Thomas was born in Melbourne, Australia and has lived there most of her life, apart from six years spent working in Europe – in Norway, France and the United Kingdom. She has been involved in education for most of her life, teaching in both primary and secondary schools. Valerie Thomas has also worked as an educational researcher and curriculum consultant, with a particular specialism in spelling.

When she isn't teaching or writing, Valerie Thomas loves travelling. She has visited most countries and continents in the world – even Antarctica – and has written about her travels and experiences. Living with a black cat helped to inspire the character of Wilbur in her *Winnie the Witch* series.

About the illustrator

Korky Paul was born in Harare, Zimbabwe, and was one of seven children. He was always interested in art, often sitting in the shade and drawing when the weather got too hot for him. His grandmother, Edith Christie, encouraged his talent and Korky Paul went on to study Fine Art at Durban Art School followed by Film Animation at the Californian Institute of the Arts.

After graduating, Korky Paul first worked in advertising before his brother convinced him to send examples of his drawings to a publishing company. Soon afterwards, he was providing the illustrations for a new picture book – *Winnie the Witch*. This series made his name and has been translated into more than 20 languages. Nowadays, the award-winning illustrator lives in Oxford and spends long holidays in Greece.

Key facts

Winnie the Witch

Author: Valerie Thomas

Illustrator: Korky Paul

First published: 1987 by Oxford University Press

Awards: Children's Book of the Year 1987

Did you know? Winnie's hat is crooked because when Korky Paul first drew her, he ran out of space on the paper and had to draw it wonky to fit it in! Korky Paul's real name is Hamish Vigne Christie Paul – Korky is his nickname.

GUIDED READING

Front cover

Show the children the front cover of *Winnie the Witch* and ask question 1 on the Guided Reading bookmark (page 10). Discuss why it might be that even though there is a witch and a cat on the front cover, the title of the story only includes the witch. Ask the children what they think the book might be about. Most children will guess it's about a witch but some might know the book(s) better and add more detail. Encourage the children to look at the smaller details. Ask: *What is happening to Winnie?* (She's falling down the stairs.) *How can you tell?* (The jugs and bottles look like they are falling over and the scrolls are flying into the air.)

Back cover

Read the children the back-cover blurb and point out the rhyming words of 'chairs' and 'stairs', 'floors' and 'doors'. Explain that the rest of the book isn't written in rhyme. Then ask them question 7 on the Guided Reading bookmark and discuss how the blurb sounds more catchy and fun with the rhyming words and might make someone want to read the book.

Finally, ask the children what adventures the witch and cat might get up to, especially since the word 'magic' is mentioned.

The first two spreads

Look at the first spread and ask the children which word is repeated (black), and why (to describe and emphasise how black and dark Winnie's house and contents are). Then discuss question 3 on the Guided Reading bookmark and discuss reasons why Winnie dresses in bright colours but her house is black. There are no right or wrong answers: maybe Winnie inherited the house; perhaps she just likes dressing in colour. Ask: *Do you think everything about a witch should be black?*

In the second spread, the author says: 'And that is how the trouble began.' Ask the children question 6 on the Guided Reading bookmark. Discuss what the trouble might be. Do the children have any ideas? Ask: *If Wilbur is as black as everything in the house – what might happen?*

Spreads 3–5

Ask the children to look at Winnie's and Wilbur's expressions and reactions whenever Winnie sits on or trips over Wilbur. Ask: *How might each character be feeling?* Possible answers could be on: Spread 3 – Wilbur's splayed limbs suggest he is alarmed and Winnie looks surprised and concerned; Spread 4 – Winnie looks surprised and panicked as she flies through the air and Wilbur's expression is sly and cheeky. Ask: *Did Wilbur mean to trip Winnie up?* On Spread 5 (left-hand page) – Winnie looks rumpled and weary, her face is wrinkly and Wilbur's ears are sticking straight up and his whiskers are very straight and his eyes are alarmed.

When discussing these spreads, refer to question 2 on the Guided Reading bookmark. Discuss the children's views as to whether they think Wilbur is as important as Winnie in the story.

Spreads 6–7

Ask question 5 on the Guided Reading bookmark and discuss whether the layout of the illustrations on these spreads helps tell the story. Spread 6: The two panels on the left show different situations where Wilbur can be seen properly now Winnie has cast this spell. Ask the children why more space might be given to the scene on the bed (perhaps because Wilbur is doing something naughty!). Spread 7: the illustrator has split the page horizontally. Ask the children why this might be (for example, it is easier to show Wilbur being removed from the house and then Winnie tripping over him). Ask the children how the illustrator shows how many times Winnie somersaults through the air (three blue loops).

Spreads 8–10

In these spreads, the author tells us about Winnie's and Wilbur's emotions. On Spread 8 Winnie is 'furious' and on Spread 10 Wilbur is 'miserable' and Winnie is 'worried'.

Ask question 9 on the Guided Reading bookmark. Do the pictures or the words show the characters' emotions better? Which do the children think? On Spread 8 Winnie looks terrifying with her angry red nose, her pointed teeth and the way the colours have been splashed on violently to show the movement of the wand. On Spread 9 Wilbur looks dejected, with his wobbly whiskers, ears pointing slightly downwards and his droopy tail. His expression is sad. Even though we can't see Winnie's face, the way she is standing with her hand on her back shows us she is worried. On Spread 10 Wilbur's embarrassment shows in how he is holding his paws to his eyes; his mouth is small and unhappy; the birds are grinning, and Winnie's long, downturned mouth looks glum. Her body language shows sadness and defeat.

Ask the children question 4 on the Guided Reading bookmark. Talk about why Winnie was first furious and then worried. (She could be frustrated with herself for not solving the problem, then upset that she had made Wilbur miserable.) Refer to question 8 on the bookmark and ask the children for synonyms for 'furious'.

Spreads 11–12

In the final two spreads, Winnie finds a solution by changing the colour of her house instead of Wilbur. Refer the children to question 10 on the Guided Reading bookmark. Discuss how the type size could be the author's way of showing that this time Winnie will be successful, or to show what a big spell Winnie is casting!

Ask the children question 11 on the bookmark. Discuss how the house has changed from the start of the book to the end. Ask the children which house they prefer. Ask: *Do you think Winnie and Wilbur are happier at the end of the story than the start?* (They seem to be happy in both settings.)

Ask the children question 12 on the Guided Reading bookmark. Ask the children what they have learned from this story – what is the message? Possible answers are:

- never give up when faced with a problem
- treat others kindly and help them if you have hurt them.

Encourage the children to think of more messages.

SCHOLASTIC
READ&RESPOND
Bringing the best books to life in the classroom

Winnie the Witch by Valerie Thomas and Korky Paul

Focus on…
Meaning

1. Why is this book called *Winnie the Witch?*
2. Do you think that Wilbur is as important a character as Winnie?
3. Why does Winnie wear lots of colours but live in a black house?
4. Who or what is Winnie furious with when she waves her wand five times?

Focus on…
Organisation

5. How does the layout of the illustrations help to tell the story?
6. What trouble might be in store for Winnie and Wilbur?

SCHOLASTIC
READ&RESPOND
Bringing the best books to life in the classroom

Winnie the Witch by Valerie Thomas and Korky Paul

Focus on…
Language and features

7. Why are there rhyming words in the blurb on the back cover?
8. Winnie is described as 'furious'. What does this mean and what other words can you think of that would fit?

Focus on…
Purpose, viewpoints and effects

9. Which shows Winnie's and Wilbur's emotions more clearly: the words or the pictures?
10. Why is the final 'Abracadabra!' in the book so large?
11. Why does the book start and finish with a large picture of Winnie's house?
12. What do you think the message of this story is?

Extract 1

- This extract is from Spread 5. Read the text aloud, pausing at full stops and commas, and emphasising sentences that end in exclamation marks.
- Ask: *Why has the author used exclamation marks in two of the sentences?* (In the first, to emphasise how spells are dramatic; in the second, to show amazement at Wilbur's colour.)
- Ask the children if the sentences would work as well with a full stop as with an exclamation mark. (In the first, the spell would feel less dramatic; in the second, it would a statement of a fact rather than an incredible thing.)
- Circle the word ABRACADABRA. Explain that writing in capital letters is another way of showing amazement or surprise or effect.
- Open the interactive activity 'Punctuation' and ask children to choose the correct punctuation from the drop-down boxes to complete the sentences.

Extract 2

- This extract is from Spread 10. Read the text aloud, then go through circling all the verbs that end in 'ed' or 'd' ('climbed', 'looked', 'laughed', 'stayed', 'loved', 'hated'). Say the verbs aloud and ask the children to repeat them.
- Explain to the children that these are regular past-tense verbs, where you add 'ed' to words that end with a consonant (such as 'climbed') and 'd' to words that end in 'e' (such as 'hated').
- To consolidate this, look at the interactive activity 'Past it'. Ask volunteers to take it in turns to drag and drop the correct ending to the verbs in the sentences on screens 1 and 2 (either 'ed' or 'd').
- Next, go to screens 3 and 4 of the interactive activity where the children have to change the past participles into the verb in the present tense, either by removing 'ed' or 'd'. The first one has been done for them as an example.

Extract 3

- This extract talks about why black cats are unpopular. Go through the points one by one, asking the children if they agree with them. Explain to the children that some of the points are based on people's opinions, not facts, so this is not a good example of a non-fiction text.
- Next, watch the media resource 'Black Cats', a video by the Cats' Protection League. This contradicts each of the points on the extract. Before you start, explain to the children what a misconception is (a mistaken or wrong belief about something).
- After watching the video, show the extract again and ask the children to discuss each of the points, linking their answers to the video. Did they change their minds at all after seeing the video? If so, why? If not, why not?
- To finish the activity, ask: *Which was your favourite part from the text or video? Why?*

Extract 1

One day, after a nasty fall, Winnie
decided something had to be done.
She picked up her magic wand,
waved it once and ABRACADABRA!
Wilbur was a black cat no longer.
He was bright green!

Extract 2

Wilbur climbed to the top of the tallest tree to hide.
He looked ridiculous and he knew it.
Even the birds laughed at him.

Wilbur was miserable.
He stayed at the top
of the tree all day
and all night.

Next morning Wilbur
was still up the tree.
Winnie was worried.
She loved Wilbur
and hated him to
be miserable.

Extract 3

Black cats – good, bad or just unpopular?
The Ancient Egyptians worshipped cats as gods – and even black cats! So why are black cats unpopular pets nowadays?

Black cats are magical
Many people in Europe in the Middle Ages (around 400 years ago) believed that black cats and witches shared a special relationship. Some people thought that witches could even turn themselves into black cats and many black cats were killed because of this.

Black cats are unlucky
In the past, some people thought it was unlucky if a black cat crossed their path in the moonlight: they believed it was a sign that there would be death in their family. Even nowadays some people still think black cats are unlucky.

Black cats are bad for selfies
Nowadays, people like to take lots of 'selfies' – photographs of themselves! They also like to take pictures of their pets and black cats do not photograph as well as cats of other colours.

Black cats are scary
Because people think that black cats are witches' pets, and because cats like to go out at night (which is scarier than daytime), they think they are scary animals.

Black cats are boring
Some cats are stripy, some are ginger, some are white and some are brown and some are all these colours. Black cats are just one colour and people think that's boring. Some animal charities say that most of their cats who cannot find homes are black in colour – you can see why!

1. Contractions

Objective

To read words with contractions and understand that the apostrophe represents the omitted letter(s).

What you need

Copy of *Winnie the Witch*, interactive activity 'Contractions: making words shorter'.

What to do

- Remind the children of what contractions are – two words that become one, with the apostrophe standing in for an omitted letter. Write one or two examples, such as *I'll* or *you've* to illustrate the point.
- Tell the children that there is one contraction in *Winnie the Witch – couldn't –* that appears on spreads 3, 4 and 7. Ask: *What are the full two words?* (could not)
- Work through screen 1 of the interactive activity 'Contractions: making words shorter', inviting individuals up to the front to match the contraction to its correct full form. Then, go through screens 2 and 3, asking for volunteers to type the correct contractions into the boxes.

Differentiation

Support: Write cards for the words in the interactive activity. Ask the children to match the contraction to the correct two words and repeat to consolidate.

Extension: Talk about how an apostrophe can also denote possession. Write sentences to practise this rule, for example:

- The book belongs to Anna
  = Anna's book
- The meowing of the cats was loud
  = The cats' meowing was loud
  (Note the plural possessive in the second example.)

Encourage the children to think of sentences when they would use the possessive apostrophe and to write them down.

2. Plurals

Objective

To add 'es' or 's' to nouns to make plurals.

What you need

Copy of *Winnie the Witch*, media resource 'Playful plurals', individual whiteboards (Extension only).

What to do

- At the start of the lesson, ask the children if they can remember how to make a regular noun plural (by adding 's' to the ending).
- Tell the class that you are going to change some of the nouns found in *Winnie the Witch* into their plural forms.
- As a group, look at the media resource 'Playful plurals' to consolidate how to change singular nouns into their plurals. Ask the children what the plural form of each item in the thumbnails is, before double-clicking on each to reveal the plural form.

Differentiation

Extension: Ask the children if they know the rule for making plurals from nouns ending in 's', 'ch', 'x', 'sh', 'z' (add 'es'). Say: *Write the plurals of the following irregular nouns on your whiteboards: witch, grass, bush, fizz, sandwich, fox, peach, mash, whiz.* You could also ask the children to try to think of their own examples to add to this list.

3. Making comparisons

Objective

To add 'er' and 'est' to adjectives where no change is needed in the spelling of root words.

What you need

Media resource 'Making comparisons'; classroom objects or soft toys (Support only).

Cross-curricular links

Science, maths

What to do

- Display the media resource 'Making comparisons'. Ask the children to work in pairs, looking at the different domestic animals on the screen.
- Using their knowledge of 'er' and 'est' suffixes (revise this if necessary), ask the children to compare the animals in size and appearance and compose their own statements. For example:
  - The horse is the largest animal.
  - The kitten is smaller than the cat.
  - The cat is furrier than the bird.
  - The goldfish is brighter than the snake.
- Ask the children to share their statements, and write these on the whiteboard.
- To increase the mathematical emphasis of the activity, you could ask the children to guess which animal would be the heaviest or lightest, and then put them in order (heaviest to lightest or vice versa).

Differentiation

Support: To help reinforce the difference between 'er' and 'est' suffixes, use classroom objects or soft toys of different heights and textures, and ask the children to line them up from the smallest to the largest, softest to hardest, and so on.

4. Feel the beat

Objective

To understand the division of words into syllables.

What you need

Copies of *Winnie the Witch*.

Cross-curricular link

Music

What to do

- Explain to the children that spoken words can be thought of as 'beats'. Words with only one syllable have one 'beat' (such as 'witch'), while words with two syllables have two 'beats' (such as 'Winnie' and 'Wilbur'). You could help the children understand this by clapping the syllables of words, and asking the children to join in too.
- Next, ask children to work in pairs and look through *Winnie the Witch* for examples of two-syllable words, writing these on their whiteboards. Examples (excluding 'Winnie' and 'Wilbur') could include: 'forest', 'outside', 'inside', 'carpets', 'blankets', 'trouble', 'began', 'couldn't', 'over', 'nasty', 'something', 'magic', 'longer', 'allowed', 'outside', 'yellow', 'purple', 'tallest', 'morning', 'hated', 'purring', 'instead', 'cushions', 'gleaming'.
- If children are unsure about the beats, they can clap out the words when sounding them out.
- Bring the class together to discover which words they have found in the book.
- Ask the children if they can give you any examples of two-beat words (or more) that they know. Alternatively, ask them if they noticed any words in the book that had more than two syllables.

Differentiation

Support: Ask the children to find single-beat words from the book.
Extension: Challenge children to find examples of words with more than two syllables in the book (for example, 'somersaults', 'furious', 'Abracadabra') or think up ones of their own.

1. Cause and effect

Objective

To predict what might happen from details stated or implied.

What you need

Copies of *Winnie the Witch*.

What to do

- As a class look at spreads 3 and 4 of *Winnie the Witch*. Draw the children's attention to the repeated phrases:
  - On the left-hand side: 'When Wilbur sat on... with his eyes open, Winnie could see him. She could see his eyes, anyway.'
  - On the right-hand side: 'But when Wilbur closed his eyes and went to sleep, Winnie couldn't see him at all. So she...'
- Explain that this is a good example of cause and effect: in the first two sentences, the author explains a situation when things are OK. Then we are shown how it can go wrong.
- Ask the children to work in pairs to come up with alternative scenarios for Winnie and Wilbur, for example: 'When Wilbur sat on the slide with his eyes open, Winnie could see him. She could see his eyes, anyway. But when Wilbur closed his eyes and went to sleep, Winnie couldn't see him at all. So she slid down the slide on top of him!'
- Bring the class back together to share their ideas.

2. My home

Objective

To link what they read to their own experiences.

What you need

Copies of *Winnie the Witch*, interactive activity 'Winnie's house', photocopiable page 20 'My home'.

Cross-curricular links

Geography, computing

What to do

- Winnie's house is described in a lot of detail in *Winnie the Witch*, particularly in spreads 1 and 12. Read these again with the children and then ask them to close their copy of the book.
- Open the interactive activity 'Winnie's house' and tell the children that they have to try to remember how the different items changed in colour from the beginning to the end by drawing a line to match them up. Ask for volunteers to do this. (Answers: the house is yellow with a red roof and red door; the chairs are white; the carpet is green with pink roses; the bed is blue; the sheets are pink and white; the blankets are pink; the bath is a gleaming white.)
- Either as homework, or as extra class work, ask children to write about their home using photocopiable page 20 'My home'. Encourage them to think carefully about the colours found in their bedroom, as well as using other adjectives, such as 'gleaming' (spread 12). There is space on the sheet for them to draw a colourful picture of their home.
- Call the class back together and ask them to present their work. Write examples of good adjectives or unusual colours and ask the children how they decided on those.

Differentiation

Extension: Encourage children to compare their home with Winnie's, using expressions such as: 'In Winnie's house, the bath was black. In mine, it is bright yellow.' 'I don't like green carpets. I prefer dark-brown floor boards.'

3. What's it all about?

Objective

To discuss their understanding of books.

What you need

A copy of *Winnie the Witch*.

Cross-curricular link

PSHE

What to do

- Ask the children to tell you what *Winnie the Witch* is about. (They will probably tell you that it's about a witch called Winnie who lives in a house where everything is black. Her cat called Wilbur is also black and because of this she always falls over him so she decides to change his colour so she can see him.)
- Agree with the children that this is what the book is about, but explain that, often, stories also have another message to tell readers. Ask the children if they can guess what this might be and how they came to this answer.
- Good answers might include: to keep looking for solutions to problems even when things keep going wrong, such as when Winnie keeps trying to change Wilbur's colour but finds that this also brings problems; the importance of thinking about other people's (or animals') feelings as well as your own, such as when Winnie feels awful about upsetting Wilbur when she turned him multicoloured and how she puts this right.
- Ask the children if they can think of examples in their own lives – such as in the playground or at home – when they have tried to solve a problem or changed their behaviour to help a friend whose feelings were hurt. Encourage the children to share their thoughts with the class.

Differentiation

Support: Ask children to tell you about any other books they have read in which the characters work together to solve a problem.
Extension: Ask children to come up with a different solution for the end of the book.

4. Meet my friend, the witch

Objective

To explain clearly their understanding of what is read to them.

What you need

Copies of *Winnie the Witch*, photocopiable page 21 'Meet my friend, the witch', drawing materials.

Cross-curricular link

Art

What to do

- Explain that much can be said about a character through their actions, rather than their words. This is particularly important in picture books, where there are fewer words to describe characters than in longer books, and where pictures are important in conveying information.
- With this in mind, ask the children to tell you what they know about Winnie from the book, both physically and personality-wise. Suggestions could include:
  - She's not a young witch (she has white hairs).
  - She seems clumsy (she's always falling over).
  - She doesn't look scary (she has a friendly face).
  - She tries to be like other witches by casting spells.
  - She's not very good at spells as they seem to go wrong.
  - She is a caring person because she hates to see Wilbur upset.
- Hand out photocopiable page 21 'Meet my friend, the witch' and ask the children to either draw their own version of Winnie or make up their own witch in the blank space. Then, using ideas from the exercise above and the book, they should write a character description on the lines below, including details like the name of their witch, age, where they live, what they like and dislike and what sort of person they are. Remind the children to use capital letters where necessary and a full stop at the end of each sentence.

5. Let's get talking

Objective

To participate in discussion about books, taking turns and listening to what others say.

What you need

Copies of *Winnie the Witch.*

Cross-curricular link

Drama

What to do

- Explain to the class that no one speaks in *Winnie the Witch* and ask if they can think of a reason why. (There is no right answer here but a possible reason could be that Winnie is human and Wilbur is a cat.)
- Ask the children to work in pairs or small groups to imagine what might be said in one of the following scenarios, using copies of the book to help them:
  - Winnie sits on or trips over Wilbur.
  - Winnie tells Wilbur to get off the bed.
  - Winnie changes Wilbur's colour.
  - The birds see Wilbur in the tree.
  - Wilbur goes back to being a black cat and comes down from the tree.
- Ask each pair or group to perform their dialogue for the class. Does the dialogue correctly describe the scenario?
- If anyone is feeling brave, they could try a monologue, speaking to the class as one character.

Differentiation

Support: Encourage children to practise having basic conversations with each other and to be aware of how they take it in turns to speak.
Extension: Ask children to write their dialogue, including as many punctuation marks as they can.

6. Put it in order!

Objective

To discuss the sequence of events in books.

What you need

Copies of *Winnie the Witch*, interactive activity 'Put it in order!'.

What to do

- Load the interactive activity 'Put it in order!'.
- Tell children that one of Winnie's spells has gone wrong and has jumbled up the correct order of events in the story. She needs their help to put it back again into the right sequence by dragging the sentences into the column on the right.
- Ask for a new volunteer for each new sentence. If the children disagree with the volunteer's decision, ask them to put their hand up to explain why.

Differentiation

Extension: Ask children to think how the story might be different if they jumble up several of the elements, particularly those in the middle. Ask them to discuss what might have happened, for example, if Wilbur had stayed with the birds.

My home

- Draw a picture of your home in the space below and then complete the sentences, using as much description as you can.

I live in a ______________________________

It is ______________________________

____

My bedroom is ______________________________

____

In my bedroom, I have ______________________________

____

Outside, ______________________________

____

Meet my friend, the witch

- Draw a picture of Winnie the Witch or a picture of a witch that you have made up.
- Write a short paragraph to describe your witch.

TALK ABOUT IT

1. Getting to know you

Objective

To participate actively in collaborative conversations, staying on topic and initiating and responding to comments.

What you need

Copies of *Winnie the Witch*, interactive activity 'Asking questions', photocopiable page 25 'Asking questions'.

What to do

- Ask the class if they know what a question looks like when it is written down.
- They should answer that it contains a question mark – if some children don't know or can't remember what one looks like, draw it on the whiteboard.
- You should also tell them that questions usually begin with certain words, for example: 'who', 'what', 'when', 'where', 'why'.
- Display the interactive activity 'Asking questions'. Ask the children to match the correct question words with the rest of the sentences. The answers are:
  - Will Wilbur forgive you for turning him pink?
  - Where did you last go on holiday?
  - Are the birds always so mean?
  - What word do you use for a magic spell?
  - Who is more clever – you or Wilbur?
  - Why was everything in your house black?
  - Where do you like to go on holiday?
  - Do you always wear stripy socks?
- Ask for someone to volunteer to be Winnie and be interviewed by others in the class using these and their own questions.
- As a homework or additional class activity, ask the children to think of questions that they would like to ask someone in a book, film or television programme. They should write these down on photocopiable page 25 'Asking questions' and then read them aloud to the class.

2. Abracadabra!

Objective

To listen and respond appropriately to others and build their vocabulary.

What you need

Copies of *Winnie the Witch*.

What to do

- Ask the children what their favourite words and expressions are. Ask what word they use when they think something is wonderful.
- Ask the children which magic word is used a lot in the book (Abracadabra!).
- Explain that magicians often use this word when they are performing tricks as a way to show that something amazing is about to happen and to get their audience excited.
- Ask the children if they know of any other magic words (examples could include 'hocus pocus', 'hey presto', 'open sesame!').
- Say that these words associated with magic often rhyme or have a punchy rhythm. Ask the children why this might be. (Possible answers could include that this makes them sound more impressive, exciting and mysterious, especially if they sound like they come from another language.)
- Ask the children to brainstorm ideas either in pairs or a small group to come up with their own words for magic tricks and spells. Encourage them to play with sounds, rhythm, alliteration and assonance to make their words (and of course remind them that the words don't need to make sense).
- Bring the class together again and ask children to share their words. Make a list of them on the whiteboard and ask them to vote for their favourites.

Differentiation

Support: Children use 'hocus pocus' as a starter word.
Differentiation: Children compose a four line spell using their 'magic' words.

3. Wilbur versus the birds

Objective

To participate in discussions, performances and role play.

What you need

Copies of *Winnie the Witch.*

Cross-curricular link

PSHE

What to do

- Split the class into small groups of no more than four or five children.
- As a class, look in detail at spread 10 of *Winnie the Witch.* Ask the children what is going on in the spread. (The birds are all laughing at Wilbur and his colour.)
- Tell the children that since there isn't any dialogue for this spread, they are going to make it up instead. One person should be Wilbur and the other the birds. Ask them to make up a short sketch on what the birds say to Wilbur when he goes into the tree and how he responds.
- Encourage the children to be creative in the language they use and to think about different scenarios.
- Bring the class back together to perform their sketches.

Differentiation

Support: Provide the children with speech starters.
Differentiation: How varied can the children make the scene? Ask confident learners if they can turn the tables completely and make Wilbur cross with the birds.

4. Face and features

Objective

To give well-structured descriptions, including for expressing feelings.

What you need

Copies of *Winnie the Witch.*

Cross-curricular links

PSHE

What to do

- Tell the children that they are going to consider how drawings convey people's feelings, often through facial expressions and body language.
- Ask the children if they can think of any examples of facial expressions or features that help to show how someone is feeling (for example, frowning eyebrows for anger or worry or confusion; big smiles for happiness) and any body language that does the same (for example, crossed arms for impatience or anger).
- Ask the children to look in detail at spread 5 of the book. Ask: *What sort of expression does Winnie have on the left-hand page and how can you tell?* (She looks frazzled, shaken, fed up – the lines on her face suggest this, and the way she is holding her head.) *What about Wilbur?* (Scared and shocked – his eyes are wide open and his whiskers very straight.)
- Then look at the right-hand page. Ask: *What are their faces and body language saying here?* (Winnie looks hopeful and rather manic – her eyes are wide open, as is her mouth, and her hair is also reflecting this. Wilbur looks worried and perhaps a little confused – his tongue is out and his eyes are starey.)
- Ask the children to choose any spread in the book and, in pairs, talk about what they think the characters are feeling and why. There is no right or wrong answer, unless, for example, they say someone is sad when they are clearly happy!

5. Is Winnie the Witch mean?

Objective

To articulate and justify answers, arguments and opinions.

What you need

Copies of *Winnie the Witch.*

Cross-curricular links

PSHE, philosophy

What to do

- Tell children that today you are going to consider whether they think Winnie the Witch was mean to Wilbur.
- Start the discussion by reviewing the events of the story: Winnie can't see Wilbur so she turns him different colours with disastrous effects until she realises the consequences of her actions.
- Ask the children to vote on whether Winnie is mean – intentionally or not – for changing Wilbur into different colours, and make a note of the numbers on the whiteboard.
- Then ask the children to justify their opinions with examples and explanations – they can use the illustrations to back up their thoughts.
- At the end of the debate, ask if anyone has changed their mind. If they have, ask them to explain why.
- Take a final vote to see if opinion has changed.

Differentiation

Extension: The children could pretend that they are in a courtroom and argue their case in front of a judge.

6. Be the narrator!

Objective

To participate in discussions and presentations.

What you need

Copies of *Winnie the Witch.*

Cross-curricular links

PSHE

What to do

- Tell the children that the story of *Winnie the Witch* isn't told by one of the characters – it's told by a separate person – a third person.
- Explain to them that if a story is told by one of the characters involved, it might have more opinions and emotions in it because the character will tell it from their point of view.
- Ask the children to work in small groups or pairs and to imagine they are telling the story from either Winnie's or Wilbur's point of view. Encourage them to think about how they might tell the story differently. For example, Winnie might get fed up with falling over Wilbur and then feel really bad when she upsets him. Wilbur might be worried every time Winnie casts a spell because she often gets it wrong!
- Ask the class to reconvene and share their versions with everyone else.

Differentiation

Support: Choose one scene from the story and ask the children to pretend to be either Wilbur or Winnie and describe what is happening.
Extension: In Winnie's house there is a portrait of a witch who looks worried (for example – spreads 5 and 12). Ask the children to present the story from her viewpoint, according to what she has seen and heard.

Asking questions

- Write down five fantastic questions that you would like to ask your favourite character from a book, film or television programme.
- In the box below, draw a picture of your character.

1. ______________________________

____

2. ______________________________

____

3. ______________________________

____

4. ______________________________

____

____

____

5. ______________________________

____

____

____

____

GET WRITING

1. Writing a sequel

Objective

To plan what they are going to write about.

What you need

Copies of *Winnie the Witch*, printable page 'Writing a sequel'.

What to do

- Ask the children: *What do you think happened next to Wilbur and Winnie?* (Some children might make suggestions based on other books in the series.) Write ideas on the whiteboard.
- Tell the children that they are going to plan a sequel to *Winnie the Witch* by completing a storyboard using pictures and captions. Their stories could perhaps pick up on something that happened in this story. Prompt with questions such as: *What if the spell broke? What if Wilbur got hold of Winnie's wand and cast his own spell?*
- Before the children start writing, recap how stories are structured: with a beginning (when characters are introduced), a middle (when most of the action happens), and an end (where everything comes together).
- Hand out copies of the printable page 'Writing a sequel'.
- Encourage the children to really use their imagination in planning a sequel and not simply retell the same story.

Differentiation

Support: Children draw the pictures for their story and include key words.
Extension: Children write a full story to accompany the pictures and captions using full sentences.

2. Animal adoption

Objectives

To use expanded noun phrases in descriptions.

What you need

Copies of *Winnie the Witch*, media resource 'Animal adoption', photocopiable page 29 'Animal adoption', paper and pencils or pens.

Cross-curricular link

Art

What to do

- Start the lesson by asking the children: *Do you know what an animal rescue centre is?* (A special adoption centre where pets stay until they can find a new home.) Ask: *Have any of you adopted pets from animal shelters?* (For example, the Blue Cross, the RSPCA, Battersea Dogs and Cats Home and so on.)
- Next, display the media resource 'Animal Adoption' and talk the children through it.
- Point out the different details it highlights, such as the pet's name, age, and what it likes and doesn't like.
- Hand out photocopiable page 29 'Animal adoption' and tell the children that they can now create their own adoption advert, either a cat like Wilbur from *Winnie the Witch* or another animal of their choice.
- Explain that, as well as the basic information, you would like the children to use noun phrases. For example, 'Jack is a brown dog with spiky fur. He likes sleeping on soft beds.'
- At the end of the activity, invite the children to share their adverts and see which animals will be adopted by whom!

Differentiation

Support: Children use the information from the media resource to complete the adoption information.
Extension: Who can make their pet sound the friendliest?

3. Spooky spellings

Objectives

To compose a sentence orally before writing it.

What you need

Copies of *Winnie the Witch*, interactive activity 'Spooky spelling', individual whiteboards or exercise books.

What to do

- Ask children: *What are the five vowels in the alphabet?* (a, e, i, o, u)
- Explain that sometimes two vowels are put together to make a certain sound (for example, 'ou' in 'mouse', 'ai' in 'hair', and 'ee' in 'bee'). Ask the class if they can think of any other examples (for example, 'ea' in 'pea', 'ie' in 'pie' and 'oa' in 'boat').
- Check to see whether the children can spot any words with two vowels in *Winnie the Witch*.
- Display the interactive activity 'Spooky Spelling' and tell the children that they have to drag and drop the correct vowels into the words from the three options given.
- Ask for a different volunteer each time to come up and complete the words.
- Display screen 3. Ask the children to work in pairs to compose a sentence for each of the five words on the screen. When they are happy with each sentence, they should write it on their whiteboards. Ask volunteers to share their sentences with the class.

Differentiation

Support: Children should say their sentences orally before writing them out, then check that the double vowel is spelled correctly.
Extension: Ask children to think of more words that have two vowels side by side and write them on their whiteboards.

4. Cat-tastic

Objective

To use subordination ('when', 'if', 'that' or 'because') and co-ordination (using 'or', 'and' or 'but').

What you need

Interactive activity 'Cat-tastic'.

Cross-curricular links

Science, history

What to do

- Ask the children what they know about cats as animals, either from having them as pets or from reading about them. Jot down their answers on the whiteboard.
- Display screen 1 of the interactive activity 'Cat-tastic', which shows a static non-fiction information text on cats. Read through it with the children and encourage them to try to remember the key facts.
- Move on to screen 2, where children must type the correct word into the sentences, choosing from the words in the box. They should do this without referring to screen 1.
- Show the children screen 3 and ask them to write their own sentences about cats in general or about Wilbur, using subordination words ('when', 'if', 'that', 'because') and co-ordination words ('or', 'and', 'but'). For example: 'When it is dark, cats like to go outside.'; 'Ancient Egyptians liked cats because they helped keep snakes away.'; 'If cats are quiet, they can catch mice and birds.'; 'A female cat can be called a 'queen' or a 'molly' but a boy cat is called a 'tom'.'

Differentiation

Support: Children write a 'because' sentence and an 'and' sentence. Encourage them to say their sentence orally first and then write it if they feel confident.
Extension: Children could write comparisons between Wilbur and other types of cat – they could look them up on the internet.

5. Cast a spell!

Objectives

To plan what they are going to write about.

What you need

Copies of *Winnie the Witch*, individual whiteboards, photocopiable page 30 'Cast a Spell!'.

Cross-curricular links

Art

What to do

- Explain to the children that witches, like magicians, are well-known for casting spells. However, in *Winnie the Witch*, we never find out what the words are to Winnie's spells, apart from the word 'Abracadabra!'.
- Explain that you would like them to come up with their own spells, either based on what happens in the book or on something else they would like to happen in their own lives.
- Tell the children: *While there is no proper way to write a spell, using rhyming words is very common and fun.* You could use the following as an example, based on spread 5:

  Your body is black
  But I'll turn it green
  So next time it's dark
  You will be seen.
- Ask the children to write their ideas on their whiteboards, including what they would like to say in their spell and any rhyming words. Encourage them to start composing their spells on the whiteboard if they feel confident.
- Next, hand out photocopiable page 30 'Cast a spell!' to the class and ask them to write their spells neatly, concentrating on good handwriting. They should only attempt this once they feel happy and confident about their spells.
- Children should also draw a picture to accompany their spell. This could make a great classroom display!

6. Letter writing

Objective

To punctuate sentences using a capital letter and a full stop.

What you need

Copies of *Winnie the Witch*, media resource 'Letter writing'.

Cross-curricular links

PSHE, art

What to do

- Ask the children if they have ever written a letter to someone well-known, such as a favourite TV character, Santa Claus, or an author.
- Explain that, today, they will pretend to write a letter either to Valerie Thomas or Korky Paul about *Winnie the Witch.*
- When writing their letter, ask them to consider what they might like to say to them, for example:
  - I liked the book because…
  - My favourite part was when…
  - I thought Winnie / Wilbur was…
  - I liked the drawings because…
  - I have a cat and it is / isn't like Wilbur because…
  - In the next book, I would love to see…
- Display the media resource 'Letter writing' and leave it on the screen as an example to refer to.
- Before and during this activity, remind children to use capital letters at the start of their sentences and full stops, question marks or exclamation marks at the end (you may wish to revise these before they start their letter writing). You could also talk about use of capital letters for proper names (for example, Winnie, Wilbur, Korky, Valerie and so on).
- Encourage the children to draw a picture from the book, if they wish, to accompany their letter.

Differentiation

Support: Encourage children to write a sentence rather than a paragraph if they find writing difficult.

Animal adoption

- Draw a picture of an animal that needs a new home.
- Write their details.

Animal: ____________________ Name: ____________________

Age: __________ Male or female: ____________________

I like: ____

I don't like: ____

My favourite food is: ____

My special talent is: ____

You should adopt me because ____________________________

____

Cast a spell!

- Now it's your turn! Write your own magic spell!

1. What happened?

Objective

To explain clearly their understanding of what is read to them.

What you need

Printable page 'What happened?', a copy of *Winnie the Witch*.

What to do

- Hand out the printable page 'What happened?' to the children and tell them that you are going to revise what they have learned from reading *Winnie the Witch*.
- Ask children to work on their own, answering the questions on the sheet to the best of their ability.
- Once the children have finished this activity, go through each question with the class, asking for answers. If children answer incorrectly, ask if someone else knows the right answer. (Answers: 1. his green eyes, which were only visible when he was awake; 2. after she had fallen down the stairs; 3. on the bed; 4. because Winnie couldn't see him in the garden/grass; 5. five times; 6. red, yellow, pink, blue and purple; 7. all day and all night; 8. yellow)

2. Sorting out the sentences

Objective

To punctuate sentences using a capital letter and a full stop.

What you need

Printable page 'Sorting out the sentences', interactive activity 'Sorting out sentences', interactive whiteboard (for support activity only).

What to do

- Ask the children what important punctuation and grammar rules they need to remember when writing a sentence (capital letters at the start, capital letters for proper nouns and full stops, or similar, at the end).
- Tell the children they are going to practise writing sentences with capital letters and full stops in the right places, and hand out printable page 'Sorting out the sentences'.
- Explain that Winnie's made another silly mistake with her wand and that the children need to put each sentence in the right order, remembering to include capitals at the beginning of sentences and for names, and full stops at the end.
- Call the class back together and go through the sentences. (Answers: 1. Everything in the house was black. 2. Winnie couldn't see Wilbur. 3. Winnie sat on Wilbur. 4. Sometimes he slept on the carpet. 5. Wilbur was not allowed on the bed. 6. Winnie fell into a rose bush. 7. The birds all laughed at him. 8. Winnie waved her wand again and again.)

Differentiation

Support: Display the interactive activity 'Sorting out the sentences' on the whiteboard and go through each one with the children, helping them to put in the correct punctuation and capital letters.
Extension: Challenge children to write their own sentences about the book, remembering to include capital letters and full stops.

3. Short and sweet

Objective

To spell by learning to spell more words with contracted forms.

What you need

Printable page 'Short and sweet', cards or sticky notes (for support only).

What to do

- Ask the children if they can remember what a contraction is. (Two words that join together to become one, often with an apostrophe to signify a missing letter.) It might be useful to give a few examples, such as: it is = it's, is not = isn't, and so on.
- Once the children have the hang of this, hand out printable page 'Short and sweet'. Explain that you want them to write the correct contractions for the two words that are printed in bold in each sentence. (Answers: 1. can't; 2. She's; 3. isn't; 4. It's; 5. They're; 6. doesn't; 7. He's; 8. They'll)
- When a suitable amount of time has passed, go through the activity with the class, asking for volunteers to give the correct answer.

Differentiation

Support: Children could play a matching game to pair the contractions with their full forms. Write the words on individual cards and their contractions on other cards and ask the children to match them up.

4. It's in the past!

Objective

To add the ending 'ed' to verbs where no change is needed to the root word

What you need

Printable page 'It's in the past!', highlighter pens, copies of *Winnie the Witch*.

What to do

- Quickly remind children that the way to make a simple past tense in regular verbs is to add the letter 'd' to any verb ending in 'e' (for example, live = lived) or to add 'ed' to verbs ending in a consonant (for example, talk – talked). See if the children can give you any more examples and write these on the board.
- Hand out the printable page 'It's in the past!' which has 13 regular past-tense verbs from *Winnie the Witch* hidden in a wordsearch grid. Ask the children to work individually, highlighting each of the words they find. To help them, the verbs have been included in the infinitive in the panel below. (Answers: lived, closed, tripped, decided, picked, waved, turned, climbed, looked, laughed, stayed, loved, hated)
- When they have finished, go through the grid on the interactive whiteboard, highlighting each word. You could either do this yourself or ask for volunteers to help.

Differentiation

Support: If children struggle with this, ask them to look through *Winnie the Witch* and make a note of any verbs that they can identify in the present or past tense.
Extension: Ask children if they can find other examples of the past tense in the book. These will be quite simple, for example: 'was', 'were', 'had', 'slept', 'sat', 'fell', 'lay' and so on, but have been excluded from the main activity because they are irregular.